Letts

CW00739188

KS2
Success

Age
7-11

Grammar
Punctuation & Spelling

Test
Practice Papers

Rachel
Axten-Higgs
and Shelley
Welsh

Contents

(pull-out section at the back of the book)

Introduction and instructions

How these tests will help your child

The practice test papers provided in this book are similar to the ones your child will take at the end of Year 6 in English grammar, punctuation and spelling. They can be used any time throughout the year to provide practice for the Key Stage 2 tests.

The results of the papers will provide a good idea of the strengths and weaknesses of your child.

Administering the tests

- Provide your child with a quiet environment where they can complete their test undisturbed.
- Provide your child with the following equipment: pen or pencil, ruler and eraser.
- The amount of time given for each test varies, so remind your child at the start of each one how long they have and give them access to a clock or watch.
- You should only read the instructions out to your child, not the actual questions.
- Although handwriting is not assessed, remind your child that their answers should be clear.

Each test is made up of two papers.

Paper 1: questions

- There are 50 questions, each worth 1 mark.
- Your child will have **45 minutes** to complete the test paper.
- There are different types of questions in this paper. The space given shows the type of answer that is needed.
  - **Multiple choice**: these questions might need lines to be drawn to the answer, a tick put next to it, or a circle put around it. Your child should read the question carefully so they know how to answer it.
  - **Short answers**: some questions have a line or box for the answer – this shows that the answer might be a word, phrase or sentence. Where there is more than one answer line, your child is expected to write a sentence or longer answer.

Paper 2: spelling

- There are 20 spellings, each worth 1 mark.
- Your child will have approximately **15 minutes** to complete the test paper.
- Using the spelling administration guide on pages 63–64, read each spelling and allow your child time to fill it in on their spelling paper.

Marking the tests

The answers and mark scheme allow you to check how your child has done. Fill in the marks that your child achieved for each part of the tests.

Please note: these tests are **only a guide** to the level or mark your child can achieve and cannot guarantee the same level is achieved during their Key Stage 2 tests.

	Set A	Set B	Set C
Paper 1: questions	/ 50	/ 50	/ 50
Paper 2: spelling	/ 20	/ 20	/ 20
Total	/ 70	/ 70	/ 70

These scores roughly correspond with these levels:

up to 24 = well below required level

25–43 = below required level

44–53 = meets required level

54–70 = exceeds required level

When an area of weakness has been identified, it is useful to go over it and to look at similar types of questions with your child. Sometimes your child will be familiar with the subject matter but might not understand what the question is asking. This will become apparent when talking to your child.

Shared marking and target setting

Engaging your child in the marking process will help them to develop a greater understanding of the tests and, more importantly, provide them with some ownership of their learning. They will be able to see more clearly how and why certain areas have been identified for them to target for improvement.

Top tips for your child

Don't make silly mistakes. Make sure you emphasise to your child the importance of reading the question. Easy marks can be picked up by just doing as the question asks.

Make answers clearly legible. If your child has made a mistake, encourage them to put a cross through it and write the correct answer clearly next to it. Encourage your child to use an eraser as little as possible.

Don't panic! These practice test papers, and indeed the end of Key Stage 2 tests, are meant to provide a guide to the level a child has attained. They are not the be-all and end-all, as children are assessed regularly throughout the school year. Explain to your child that there is no need to worry if they cannot do a question – tell them to go on to the next question and come back to the problematic question later if they have time.

Paper 1: questions

- Your **grammar**, **vocabulary** and **punctuation** will be tested in this task.
- You will be given **45 minutes** to complete this task.

---

1   Insert the **capital letters** and **full stops** in the passage below.

the school was closed because of the snow the children didn't mind the

teachers worked at home but the children played outside

1 mark

---

2   Which pair of **pronouns** is best to complete the sentence below?

The dog chased _____ down the road. _____

ran very fast because we were scared.

Tick one.

I	She	☐
her	He	☐
us	We	☐
them	They	☐

1 mark

---

3   Circle all the **nouns** in the sentence below.

The sun shone through the trees onto the car.

1 mark

---

4 Circle the **preposition** in the sentence below.

The hurdler jumped over the hurdles.

1 mark

5 Which sentence uses a **comma** correctly?

Tick **one**.

Before, the end of the game the opposition left the pitch. ☐

Before the end of the game, the opposition left the pitch. ☐

Before the end of the game the opposition, left the pitch. ☐

Before the end of the game the opposition left, the pitch. ☐

1 mark

6 Draw lines to match the words with their most likely final punctuation. Use each punctuation mark once.

Sentence	Punctuation
Help	.
Where is your house	?
I had toast for breakfast	!

1 mark

7 Tick one box to show where the missing **question mark** should go.

Chris asked, "How many days until my birthday" as he looked at the calendar.

☐ ☐ ☐ ☐

1 mark

6

8

Change the **question** in the table below into a **command**.
Write the command in the box.

Question	Command
Can you stop and listen to me?	

1 mark

9

Rewrite this sentence using a **colon** and **bullet points**.

We packed our bags with the following swimsuits, goggles, beach towels

and sun cream.

_____

_____

_____

_____

_____

1 mark

10

Put a tick in each row to show whether each underlined word in this
sentence is a **noun** or an **adjective**.

I helped the chatty little girl to play on the swings.

	Noun	Adjective
chatty		
girl		
swings		

1 mark

11 Complete the sentence below with a **contraction** that makes sense.

If you tell us what to buy _____ go shopping for you!

1 mark

12 Put a tick in each row to show whether the sentence is a **statement**, a **command**, an **exclamation** or a **question**.

Sentence	Statement	Command	Exclamation	Question
Wash the dishes.				
Where is the sink?				
The dishes are dirty.				
Ouch, that water is hot!				

1 mark

13 Which sentence contains two **verbs**?

Tick **one**.

Jacob packed his bag and ran to school. ☐

Tiegan ran happily and joyously to school. ☐

Jasmin packed her bag with toys and games. ☐

The phone rang in the hallway. ☐

1 mark

14 Find one word that can complete **both** sentences below.

The dog let out a _____ when it saw the cat.

The girl took a rubbing from the _____ of the tree.

1 mark

15 Complete the sentences below using either I or me.

_____ went to the shops.

Fred and _____ played a board game.

He came with _____ to talk to my teacher.

The dog barked loudly at Joe and _____.

I had to put my hand up before the teacher would help _____.

1 mark

16 Which two sentences below should end with a **full stop**?

Tick **two**.

Help, call the police ☐

I like horse riding because it is fun ☐

Do I have to go to the shops with you ☐

Computers make it quicker to produce long texts ☐

1 mark

17 Circle all the **adverbs** in the sentence below.

The mouse scuttled quickly and silently across the floor.

1 mark

18 Put a tick in each row to show whether the underlined words are **main**, **subordinate** or **relative clauses**.

Sentence	Main clause	Subordinate clause	Relative clause
My friend is coming round <u>because we are doing our homework</u> together.			
My friend, <u>who is called Sarah</u>, makes me laugh.			
<u>My friend Alice came for tea</u> as her mum was ill.			

1 mark

19 Circle the **conjunction** in the sentence below.

Despite the bad weather, the Summer Fair raised a lot of money for new sports equipment.

1 mark

20 Which two of these sentences are **statements**?

Tick **two**.

How long until playtime? ☐

Playtime lasts for 15 minutes. ☐

Go out to play now! ☐

Playtime is in the morning. ☐

Is there a playtime in the afternoon? ☐

1 mark

21 Write a **contraction** to replace the underlined words in each sentence below.

We are going on holiday in the summer.

$\downarrow$

They have not got any books left in the shop.

$\downarrow$

1 mark

22 Rewrite the sentence below as **direct speech**.
Remember to punctuate your answer correctly.

The teacher told the children to put their coats on and go out to play.

_____

_____

1 mark

23 Write two **adjectives** to complete the sentence below.

The _____ dog bit the leg of the _____ man.

1 mark

24 Choose a **synonym** for lovely in the sentence below and write it in the box.

The princess looked lovely in her dress.

$\downarrow$

1 mark

25 Write a sentence using the word book as a **noun**.
Remember to punctuate your answer correctly.

_____

Write a sentence using the word book as a **verb**.
Remember to punctuate your answer correctly.

_____

1 mark

26 Underline the **subordinate clause** in each sentence below.

After the race had finished, the two drivers shook hands.

The children filed into the classroom because the bell had rung.

Although they were tired, the children kept running.

1 mark

27 Tick the words that are **antonyms** of beautiful.

Tick **one**.

pretty, lovely   ☐

unattractive, unsightly   ☐

difficult, hard   ☐

plentiful, bountiful   ☐

1 mark

28 Put a **prefix** at the beginning of each word to make it mean the opposite.

_____ active

_____ stable

_____ similar

1 mark

29 What does the root <u>rupt</u> mean in the word family below?

interrupt   **disrupt**   **erupt**

Tick **one**.

evolve ☐

break ☐

finish ☐

annoy ☐

1 mark

30 Insert a pair of **dashes** to show **parenthesis** in the sentence below.

My brother the one who is mad about music is going to a music festival this weekend.

1 mark

31 Circle one of the following suffixes to make <u>soft</u> an **adverb**.

-ness   -ly   -er   -est

1 mark

32 Which sentence uses a **colon** correctly?

Tick **one**.

We had to buy the following: jam, butter, cream and scones. ☐

We had to buy: the following, jam, butter, cream and scones. ☐

We had to buy the following jam: butter, cream and scones. ☐

We had: to buy the following jam, butter, cream and scones. ☐

1 mark

33 Complete the sentence below using the **past progressive verb form** of have.

We _____ a great time in the swimming pool.

1 mark

34 Write the correct **plural form** in each space below.
One has been done for you.

one duck, three ducks

one leaf, three _____

one sheep, two _____

one box, four _____

one child, a group of _____

1 mark

35 Change all the verbs to the correct **tense**.
One has been done for you.

Yesterday the newspaper <u>is reporting</u> the results from last weekend.

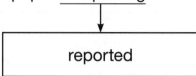

The children went on a visit yesterday and they <u>will buy</u> some souvenirs.

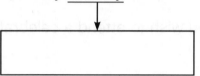

After school, Elisa will run to the bus stop so she <u>caught</u> the early bus.

_____
1 mark

36 Put a tick to show whether the **apostrophe** in each sentence is used to show **contraction** or **possession**.

Sentence	Apostrophe to show **contraction**	Apostrophe to show **possession**
Sam's bike was lying on the ground.		
You're all stars!		
It was Ryan's turn next.		

_____
1 mark

37 Label the boxes with **A (verb)**, **B (adjective)**, **C (noun)** and **D (adverb)** to show the **word class**.

The loudest lion was obviously the smallest!

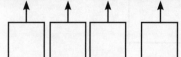

_____
1 mark

38 Rewrite this sentence using **Standard English**.

I don't want no help.

_____

39 Rewrite this sentence in an **informal** way.

Would you wish to attend a celebration at my house?

_____

40 Which of the sentences below uses **brackets** correctly?

Tick **one**.

Natasha (my best friend) came to my house for a sleepover. ☐

Natasha my (best friend) came to my house for a sleepover. ☐

(Natasha my best friend) came to my house for a sleepover. ☐

Natasha (my best friend came to my house) for a sleepover. ☐

41 Write the **homophone** for each of the following words.

ate	
weight	
sail	

42 Circle the **determiner** in each sentence below.

Before the concert they all worked hard.

We went on a noisy, scary ride.

I had to put up an umbrella because it was raining.

1 mark

43 Tick one option to complete the sentence below.

The parents and children listened _____ the head teacher

welcomed them.

Tick **one**.

between ☐

while ☐

as well as ☐

during ☐

1 mark

44 Replace the underlined words in the sentences below with a suitable **pronoun**.

Our school is really great. We are proud of <u>our school</u>.

┌─────────────────┐
│   │
└─────────────────┘

Ryan is playing happily in the park but <u>Ryan</u> must leave for home shortly.

┌─────────────────┐
│   │
└─────────────────┘

1 mark

45 Write a **question** beginning with the words below.

How often _____

_____

1 mark

46 Put a tick in each row to show whether the underlined part of the sentence is a **phrase** or a **clause**.

Sentence	Phrase	Clause
<u>The old lady</u> crossed the road.		
<u>They had fun</u> playing in the park.		
The children ran <u>so they could stretch their legs.</u>		
The snake slithered <u>in his humid tank.</u>		

1 mark

47 Rewrite this sentence in the **passive voice**.

The dog ate the bone.

_____

1 mark

48 Which of the sentences below uses a **semi-colon** correctly?

Tick **one**.

The wind was; very strong the kite flew high in the sky. ☐

The wind was very strong; the kite flew high in the sky. ☐

The wind was very strong, the kite; flew high in the sky. ☐

The wind was very strong, the kite flew; high in the sky. ☐

1 mark

49 Tick one box in each row to show whether the word after is used as a **subordinating conjunction** or a **preposition** in the sentences below.

Sentence	After as a subordinating conjunction	After as a preposition
After I brushed my teeth, I went downstairs.		
I ran after the bus but it didn't stop.		
After 9 o'clock we are ready to go to assembly.		

1 mark

50 Complete the sentence below so that it is in the **subjunctive mood**.

If it _____ to rain, we would have to cancel the race.

1 mark

Paper 2: spelling

- Your **spelling** will be tested in this task.
- There are 20 spellings and you will hear each spelling three times.
- This section should take approximately **15 minutes** to complete, although you will be allowed as much time as you need.

N.B.: The answer lines only are given below. You will need to ask someone to read the instructions and sentences to you. These can be found on page 63.

---

1 I am learning to play the _____.

2 We were _____ on the train.

3 The _____ were playing on the carpet.

4 The snake _____ loudly in his tank.

5 The explosion caused great _____.

6 The cow gave birth to two _____.

7 Sam mixed _____ into his cake mixture.

8 Max chose to _____ with Tom's game.

9 Freya's favourite animal at the zoo was the _____.

10 The man had a very successful _____ in the city.

---

11 We watched the film at the _____.

12 The children _____ out to play.

13 Howard Carter was proud to _____ the tomb.

14 The children responded to the _____ by improving their work.

15 Superman was _____ Clark Kent.

16 My uncle went to an exhibition of _____ paintings.

17 Matilda won the _____ race on sports day.

18 The children were learning about _____ in maths.

19 Mark ran quickly up the _____.

20 The _____ building is in London.

Paper 1: questions

- Your **grammar**, **vocabulary** and **punctuation** will be tested in this task.
- You will be given **45 minutes** to complete this task.

1 Find one word that can complete **both** sentences below.

I needed to _____ my laces as they had come undone.

The man put his _____ around his neck.

1 mark

2 Put a tick in each row to show whether each underlined word is an **adverb** or an **adjective**.

I ran happily through the scary woods.

	Adverb	Adjective
happily		
scary		

1 mark

3   Which of these should be written as two separate **sentences**?

Tick **one**.

My rabbit is called Flopsy and my guinea pig is called Jenny. ☐

I am good at writing but I am better at maths. ☐

Mrs James is my teacher she makes learning fun. ☐

I like horse riding because it is exciting! ☐

1 mark

4   Circle the **preposition** in the sentence below.

The children had to trudge through the mud.

1 mark

5   Write a **question** that would provide the answer below.

Question	Answer
	I would prefer to go to the park.

1 mark

6   Which two of these sentences are **statements**?

Tick **two**.

How many toys do you have? ☐

I have 15 different toys. ☐

Don't show off. ☐

Do you have a favourite toy? ☐

My favourite toy is my Batman one. ☐

1 mark

7 Which of the sentences below uses **brackets** correctly?

Tick **one**.

Ring me at home (you have my number) so we can chat. ☐

Ring me (at home you have my number) so we can chat. ☐

Ring me at home you have my number (so we can chat). ☐

(Ring me) at home you have my number so we can chat. ☐

1 mark

8 Draw lines to match each sentence with the correct final punctuation.

Sentence	Punctuation
How old are you	!
Good gracious	.
I am eight years old	?

1 mark

9 Explain how the **comma** in each of the sentences below changes the meaning to avoid **ambiguity**.

My favourite pastimes are cooking, my pets and painting.

My favourite pastimes are cooking my pets and painting.

_____

_____

1 mark

10 Change the question in the table below into a **command**.

Question	Command
Please can you tidy your room?	

1 mark

11 Put a tick in each row to show whether the word is a **noun** or a **verb**.

One has been done for you.

	Noun	Verb
tree	✓	
to skip		
hoped		
car		

1 mark

12 Circle the **adjective** in the sentence below that shows a **comparison** between the two dogs.

The larger dog yapped at the spindly legs of the little dog.

1 mark

13 Put a tick in each row to show whether the sentence is a **statement**, a **command** or a **question**.

Sentence	Statement	Command	Question
Can you listen please			
I am listening to the teacher			
Stop and listen			

1 mark

14 Which sentence uses the **hyphen** correctly?

Tick **one**.

We saw a man eating-shark at the aquarium. ☐

We saw a man-eating shark at the aquarium. ☐

We saw a man-eating-shark at the aquarium. ☐

We saw a man eating shark at-the-aquarium. ☐

1 mark

15 Change all the verbs from the **past** tense to the **present** tense.

I jumped out of bed and ran to the bathroom.

[ ]   [ ]

I reversed out of the drive and into a ditch!

[ ]

Lily had tripped over a large boulder.

[ ]

1 mark

16 Choose a **conjunction** from the box to complete the sentences below.
Use each word once.

| and | however | because |

The children were moaning _____ they did not agree with

wearing school uniform. Jake, _____, said that he did like

wearing uniform _____ disliked weekends when he had to

choose his clothes.

1 mark

17 Which word completes the sentence below so that it is grammatically correct?

The house was _____ by the builders.

Tick one.

builded ☐

built ☐

build ☐

billed ☐

1 mark

18 Complete the sentences below using either <u>I</u> or <u>me</u>.

I asked my brother to stop bothering _____.

Before the end of the day, the teacher told _____ that I had

worked hard.

My teacher gave Ryan and _____ extra homework.

Amy and _____ went to the cinema.

1 mark

19 Insert the missing **inverted commas** in the sentence below.

When you are in a library, said the librarian, you must be silent.

1 mark

20 Which pair of **pronouns** is best to complete the sentence below?

_____ needed to go to the shops for my mum as

_____ had broken her leg.

Tick **one**.

I	she	☐
her	He	☐
We	us	☐
them	They	☐

1 mark

21 Circle the **fronted adverbial** and the **adverb** in the sentence below.

Every day, Freya practises hard for the swimming competition.

1 mark

22 Which sentence contains two **verbs**?

Tick **one**.

Sam hugged his poorly sister gently but carefully. ☐

The computer whirred noisily on the desk. ☐

The child jumped and screamed in anger. ☐

Maisie skipped joyfully to school. ☐

1 mark

23 Put a tick in each row to show whether the underlined words are **main**, **subordinate** or **relative clauses**.

Sentence	Main clause	Subordinate clause	Relative clause
The animals stayed inside <u>because it was snowing outside.</u>			
The baby, <u>who was screaming loudly,</u> would not go to sleep.			
Before school started, <u>I went to the gym to do some exercise.</u>			
<u>I cleaned up my bedroom,</u> after my mum had asked me to.			

1 mark

24 Write a **contraction** to replace the underlined words in each sentence below.

<u>They are</u> going skiing in the winter.

↓

☐

We <u>will not</u> be able to go to the party.

↓

☐

1 mark

25 Which of the sentences below uses a **question mark** correctly?

Tick **one**.

"How much further do I have to cycle," moaned Tamzin? ☐

"How much further? Do I have to cycle" moaned Tamzin. ☐

"How much further do I have to cycle." moaned Tamzin? ☐

"How much further do I have to cycle?" moaned Tamzin. ☐

1 mark

26 In the sentence below, replace the word <u>said</u> with a suitable **synonym**.

"Land ahoy!" <u>said</u> the captain as he looked out to sea.

[   ]

1 mark

27 Write two sentences to show two **different** meanings of the word <u>ring</u>.

_____

_____

_____

_____

1 mark

28 Write the **homophone** for each of the following words.

mail		

hole		

bear		

1 mark

29 Tick the words that are **antonyms** of <u>tough</u>.

Tick **one**.

rough, hard ☐

mean, aggressive ☐

strong, hardy ☐

fragile, delicate ☐

1 mark

30 Label the boxes with **A (verb)**, **B (adjective)**, **C (noun)** and **D (adverb)** to show the **word class**.

The excited child talked loudly!

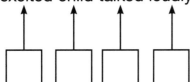

1 mark

31 Put a **prefix** at the beginning of each word to make it mean the opposite.

_____ easy

_____ mature

_____ agree

1 mark

32 Put a tick to show whether the **apostrophe** in each sentence is used to show **contraction** or **possession**.

Sentence	Apostrophe to show **contraction**	Apostrophe to show **possession**
You'll need to work hard today!		
I won't be able to help you.		
Claire's work is the best!		

1 mark

33 Insert a pair of **commas** to show **parenthesis** in this sentence.

The children all aged four went on a visit to the zoo.

1 mark

34 Underline two **adverbs** that tell you more about the **adjectives** in the sentence below.

Although Matilda's homework was very difficult, she produced a really excellent piece of writing.

1 mark

35 Add a **suffix** to each word to make an **adjective**.

friend _____   beauty _____

child _____   craze _____

1 mark

36

Each of the sentences below contains a **modal verb**.
Which event is **most likely** to happen?

Tick **one**.

I might come to your house later on. ☐

You ought to practise your piano more often. ☐

I will be at football training at 9:00 am sharp. ☐

The weather forecast says it may snow later. ☐

1 mark

37

Rewrite this sentence using correct punctuation.
One has been done for you.

W
when i wake up in the morning i have a shower after that i have

my breakfast

_____

_____

1 mark

38

Replace the underlined words with a suitable **pronoun**.

We heard James sing on stage last week and have listened to James many

times since. James is one of the best!

1 mark

34

39 Complete the sentence below with a **contraction** that makes sense.

I am sorry but I _____ be able to come to your party.

40 Rewrite this sentence using **Standard English**.

I should of done my homework last night.

_____

41 Circle the **determiner** in each sentence below.

The window was mended at last.

It was an unfortunate mistake.

I saw a lion when I was on holiday.

42 Rewrite this sentence inserting a **colon** and **commas** in the correct places.

In my bag I packed a towel a hairbrush a swimming costume and a

bottle of shampoo.

_____

_____

_____

43 Put a tick in each row to show whether the underlined part of the sentence is a **phrase** or a **clause**.

Sentence	Phrase	Clause
<u>The news spread</u> quickly on the internet.		
The noisy children played <u>in the park</u>.		
To get away from the lion, <u>the animals stampeded</u>.		
<u>The unhappy baby</u> screamed in the wooden cot.		

1 mark

44 Insert a **semi-colon** into the sentence below.

It's been hot and sunny all day we just hope it stays that way.

1 mark

45 Which option from the box below completes the sentence so that it uses the **subjunctive mood**?

was	could be	may be	were

My mum read me a fantastic fairy story. If only it _____ true!

1 mark

46 Insert a **possessive pronoun** into the sentence below.

My coat is green but _____ is blue.

1 mark

47 Insert the correct **subordinating conjunction** to complete this sentence?

| despite | because | although | nevertheless |

We played outside for hours _____ the weather was awful.

1 mark

48 Change the underlined words to show **possession**.

The <u>circus</u> new show had to be cancelled. The <u>children</u> disappointment

was clear to see. Soon the children were walking home, holding their

<u>parents</u> hands.

1 mark

49 Rewrite the sentence below as **direct speech**.
Remember to punctuate your answer correctly.

Our coach asked us if we could do an extra training session before the final.

_____

_____

1 mark

50 Put a pair of **dashes** into this sentence to show **parenthesis**.

My mum's sister currently working in the fashion industry has met

many celebrities.

1 mark

Paper 2: spelling

- Your **spelling** will be tested in this task.
- There are 20 spellings and you will hear each spelling three times.
- This section should take approximately **15 minutes** to complete, although you will be allowed as much time as you need.

> **N.B.: The answer lines only are given below. You will need to ask someone to read the instructions and sentences to you. These can be found on pages 63–64.**

1 The _____ pumps blood around the body.

2 The hare is _____ than the tortoise.

3 Sir Lancelot was a brave _____.

4 The fisherman _____ the size of the fish he caught.

5 The elephant is a large _____.

6 I made green tomato _____ to have with cheese.

7 The plot to rob the bank was _____ by the police.

8 To read a map successfully, you need to know what the _____ mean.

9 Two _____ make a whole.

10 The couple _____ in a church.

11 A _____ is a 3-D shape.

12 Matthew's car stopped _____.

13 Ian was proud of the _____ he had grown.

14 Wallace and Gromit is a funny _____.

15 The children _____ talking when the teacher entered the room.

16 There are 1,000 metres in a _____.

17 The athlete _____ the world record in the 100 m sprint.

18 The shop assistant had to clean up a spillage in the drinks _____.

19 The ladies' toilet was already _____.

20 The baby _____ started to cry when she was put to bed.

Paper 1: questions

- Your **grammar**, **vocabulary** and **punctuation** will be tested in this task.
- You will be given **45 minutes** to complete this task.

1   Circle all the **adjectives** in the sentence below.

The   kind   lady   helped   the   old   dog   over   the   uneven   ground.

1 mark

2   Circle the **four** words in the sentence below that should start with a capital letter.

For one of the words you have identified, explain why it needs a capital letter.

josh is travelling to london on the train next tuesday to visit samuel.

Word chosen _____

Why does this word need a capital letter?

_____

1 mark

3   Complete the sentences below using either <u>I</u> or <u>me</u>.

Tim and _____ went to the shops.

Finally it was my turn and _____ had to perform to

the audience.

The coach told Sarah and _____ to practise more.

My parents were very proud of _____.

1 mark

4 Rewrite the sentence below, inserting the missing **question mark**.

"Do I have to go to school today" moaned Simon.

_____

1 mark

5 Put a tick in each row to show whether the sentence is a **statement**, a **command** or a **question**.

Sentence	Statement	Command	Question
I like eating pasta			
Cook the pasta			
Which pasta is your favourite			

1 mark

6 Write a **homophone** for each of the following words.

pear		
groan		
bear		

1 mark

7 Underline the **adverb** that tells you more about the **adjective** in the sentence below.

After dinner, we had a truly amazing dessert!

1 mark

8 Which pair of **pronouns** is best to complete the sentence below?

It is time for _____ to perform _____ musical piece.

Tick **one**.

I	she	☐
her	He	☐
her	her	☐
them	They	☐

1 mark

9 Circle all the **adverbs** in the sentences below.

Mournfully, Zac trudged to boring school. He angrily kicked a rusty

can that was on the pavement.

1 mark

10 Complete the sentences below using either <u>run</u> or <u>ran</u>.

I can _____ fast.

The child _____ to school.

Jake _____ as fast as he was able to.

The children _____ quickly during the race last week.

1 mark

11   Which of the sentences below is punctuated correctly?

Tick **one**.

We packed lots of things (including the map) for our journey. ☐

We packed (lots of things including the map) for our journey. ☐

We packed (lots of things) including the map for our journey. ☐

(We packed lots of things) including the map for our journey. ☐

1 mark

12   Put a tick in each row to show whether each underlined word in the sentence below is an **adverb** or a **verb**.

I <u>shouted</u> <u>loudly</u> because I <u>was</u> lost.

	Verb	Adverb
shouted		
loudly		
was		

1 mark

13   Write a sentence that ends with an **exclamation mark**.

_____

1 mark

14   Circle the most suitable **conjunction** to complete the sentence below.

although   because   yet   finally

The children ran for shelter _____ it started to rain.

1 mark

15 Circle the two **verbs** in the sentence below.

The colourful ball broke the window as it flew through the air.

1 mark

16 Change all the **verbs** from the **present** tense to the **future** tense.

I am running to school so that I am early.

George is training hard.

The cows jump over the moon!

1 mark

17 Draw a line to match each sentence with the correct **verb**.

Sentence	**Verb**
The lions _____ eating their dinner.	has
Brookside School _____ won the cup.	have
Jason and I _____ fallen off our bikes.	are

1 mark

18 Which sentence uses a **comma** correctly?

Tick **one**.

Suddenly there was, silence in the stadium. ☐

Suddenly, there was silence in the stadium. ☐

Suddenly there was silence, in the stadium. ☐

Suddenly there, was silence in the stadium. ☐

1 mark

19 Turn these **nouns** into **noun phrases** by adding additional information.

Noun	Noun phrase
butterfly	
sky	

1 mark

20 Put a circle around the words that should have a **capital letter**.

tim, chris and kierton had all been friends since they

started willowbank.

1 mark

21 Label the boxes with **A (verb)**, **B (adjective)**, **C (proper noun)** and **D (adverb)** to show the **word class**.

We went happily on holiday to sunny Spain.

1 mark

45

22 Write a sentence that ends with **ellipses** to build suspense for your reader.

_____

1 mark

23 Change the question in the table below into a **command**.
Write the command in the box.

Question	Command
Can you help me make the lunch?	

1 mark

24 Rewrite the following sentence in the **passive voice**.

The firemen rescued the children.

_____

1 mark

25 Rewrite this sentence inserting **speech marks** in the correct places.

I wish it was the end of school, whined Tom, because I am going to

play football.

_____

_____

_____

1 mark

26 Rewrite this sentence using **Standard English**.

I ain't never going back.

_____

1 mark

27 Tick the words that are **antonyms** of <u>bright</u>.

Tick **one**.

dark, dreary   ☐

blazing, brilliant   ☐

radiant, polished   ☐

vivid, twinkling   ☐

1 mark

28 Underline the **fronted adverbial** in this sentence.

After a period of time, the sea calmed and the sun came out.

29 Tick one box in each row to show whether the **apostrophe** in each sentence is used to show **contraction** or **possession**.

Sentence	Apostrophe to show **contraction**	Apostrophe to show **possession**
Maya's coat is on the peg.		
Nick's digger is in the sandpit.		
They'll have to tidy up later!		

30 Put a tick in each row to show whether the underlined words are **main**, **subordinate** or **relative clauses**.

Sentence	Main clause	Subordinate clause	Relative clause
My bike, <u>which goes very fast</u>, is shiny and new.			
My bike is shiny and new, <u>although I know it won't be long before I scratch it!</u>			
<u>My bike is shiny</u> even though it is second-hand.			

31 Which sentence uses a **colon** correctly?

Tick **one**.

To make the model I needed the following: glue, paint and card. ☐

To make the model I needed the following glue: paint and card. ☐

To make the model: I needed the following glue, paint and card. ☐

To make the model I needed the following glue, paint and: card. ☐

1 mark

32 Write a **contraction** to replace the underlined words in each sentence below.

I should not have any more pudding!

☐

It will be alright on the night!

☐

1 mark

33 Insert four **commas** in the correct places in the sentence below.

In my school bag I have a maths book a pencil case a coat a

plastic frog and a pair of glasses.

1 mark

34 Add a **suffix** to this word to make an **adjective**.

dread = _____

1 mark

35 Circle the **determiner** in each sentence below.

An ostrich was running around.

The park was closed today.

I wanted a computer for Christmas.

1 mark

36 Which two of these sentences are **statements**?

Tick **two**.

I am very hungry. ☐

Help! I need food! ☐

Why did you not eat breakfast? ☐

How long until lunchtime? ☐

Dinner is my favourite meal of the day. ☐

1 mark

37 Insert a pair of **brackets** in the following sentence.

My friends Jake and Max came to my house for a sleepover.

1 mark

38 Write a **question** beginning with the words below.

Who is _____

1 mark

39 Rewrite this passage using correct punctuation.

it had been many years since oxford had won the race they have been

working extra hard this year

_____

_____

_____

40 Circle the **preposition** in the sentence below.

The bear was hiding in the cave.

41 Put a **prefix** at the beginning of each word to make it mean the opposite.

_____ afraid

_____ comfort

_____ probable

42 Complete the sentence below with a **contraction** that makes sense.

I _____ like eating sprouts, even at Christmas!

43 Put a tick in each row to show whether the underlined part of the sentence is a **phrase** or a **clause**.

Sentence	Phrase	Clause
The phone beeped <u>in the silent room</u>.		
<u>The mouse squeaked</u> in his house.		
The quiet baby slept <u>all day long</u>.		
They went into town <u>so they could buy some food</u>.		

1 mark

44 Which word is closest in meaning to <u>scoured</u> in the sentence below?

They <u>scoured</u> the school for the boy.

Tick **one**.

built ☐

searched ☐

taught ☐

opened ☐

1 mark

45 Each of the sentences below contains a **modal verb**.
Which event is **least likely** to happen?

Tick **one**.

My dad may take the day off tomorrow. ☐

I can't take you to your tennis lesson. ☐

We should go for a long walk when the rain stops. ☐

It looks like it might rain. ☐

1 mark

46 Which option from the box below completes the sentence so that it uses the **subjunctive mood**?

| was | might be | could be | were |

If only I _____ rich enough to sail a yacht around

the Caribbean!

1 mark

47 Rewrite what the boy is saying in this sentence as **direct speech**.
Remember to punctuate your answer correctly.

The boy said we will find the museum at the end of the next road,

on the left-hand side.

_____

_____

1 mark

48 Write **two** more words that belong to this **word family**.

circle _____ _____

49 Insert a pair of **dashes** into this sentence to show **parenthesis**.

My best friend originally from Australia knows lots of facts about wallabies.

50 Draw a line to match each **prefix** to its meaning.

aqua		two
bi		self
tele		water
auto		distant

Paper 2: spelling

- Your **spelling** will be tested in this task.
- There are 20 spellings and you will hear each spelling three times.
- This section should take approximately **15 minutes** to complete, although you will be allowed as much time as you need.

N.B.: The answer lines only are given below. You will need to ask someone to read the instructions and sentences to you. These can be found on page 64.

---

1 The children used a _____ stick to draw a line.

2 The _____ dropped the stolen vase in their rush to escape.

3 The school _____ welcomed the visitors.

4 A line of _____ were led along the beach.

5 Margaret enjoys ballroom _____.

6 I bought a green _____ for my father.

7 Howard Carter entered the _____ cautiously.

8 She bought a _____ pack of crisps.

9 Flying is the _____ way to travel to New York from England.

10 I was the _____ child in my class to get chickenpox.

---

11 Shoes are _____ on the beach.

12 The church service included a _____.

13 The giraffe has an _____ long neck.

14 Philip _____ his bag home from school.

15 Your birthday _____ on the same date every year.

16 They were _____ to reach the South Pole.

17 Jemima was _____ her pocket money to buy an action figure.

18 Grandpa was _____ wood for the fire.

19 Children _____ from regular exercise.

20 Paul staggered under the _____ of the suitcase.

Answers

General guidance to marking the questions

- Do not award a mark if more than the required number of responses have been given, e.g. more boxes ticked, more words circled, etc.
- **Underlining**: do not award a mark for a response in which only part of the required text, or less than half of a required word, is underlined, or if any additional words have been underlined.
- **Circling**: do not award a mark if the correct answer has been circled together with surrounding words.
- **Labelling**: do not award a mark if there is any ambiguity in labelling.
- **Correct answer but incorrect spelling**: if no specific mark scheme is given for spelling, incorrect spellings can be given the mark(s) as long as the meaning is clear. The exception, however, is when marking contractions, which must have correct spelling and placement of apostrophes.
- **Correct answer crossed out**: if the correct answer has been crossed out but hasn't been replaced with an alternative answer, it can be marked. But if the correct answer has been crossed out and has been replaced with another answer, the crossed-out work cannot be marked.
- **More than one answer given**: if all answers given are correct (according to the mark scheme) the mark can be awarded. If both correct and incorrect responses are given, no marks can be given.

Set A

Paper 1: questions

1. The school was closed because of the snow. The children didn't mind. The teachers worked at home but the children played outside.

    (1 mark: award 1 mark for all six correct punctuation marks)

2. us   We ✓ **(1 mark)**
3. (sun) (trees) (car)

    (1 mark: award 1 mark for all three correct)

4. (over) **(1 mark)**
5. Before the end of the game, the opposition left the pitch. ✓ **(1 mark)**

6. Help!; Where is your house?; I had toast for breakfast.

    (1 mark: award 1 mark for all three correct)

7. Chris asked, "How many days until my birthday?" as he looked at the calendar. ↑✓

    (1 mark)

8. Stop and listen to me! / Stop and listen to me.

    (1 mark)

9. We packed our bags with the following:
    - swimsuits
    - goggles
    - beach towels
    - sun cream

    (1 mark: one colon and four bullet points need to be used to gain 1 mark)

10.

	Noun	Adjective
chatty		✓
girl	✓	
swings	✓	

    (1 mark: award 1 mark for all three correct)

11. we'll **(1 mark)**

12.

Sentence	Statement	Command	Exclamation	Question
Wash the dishes.		✓		
Where is the sink?				✓
The dishes are dirty.	✓			
Ouch, that water is hot!			✓	

    (1 mark: award 1 mark for all four correct)

13. Jacob packed his bag and ran to school. ✓

    (1 mark)

14. bark **(1 mark)**
15. I; I; me; me; me

    (1 mark: award 1 mark for all five correct)

16. I like horse riding because it is fun ✓

    Computers make it quicker to produce long texts ✓

    (1 mark: award 1 mark for both correct)

17. (quickly) (silently)

    (1 mark: award 1 mark for both correct)

18.

Sentence	Main clause	Subordinate clause	Relative clause
My friend is coming round because we are doing our <u>homework together</u>.		✓	
My friend, <u>who is called Sarah</u>, makes me laugh.			✓
<u>My friend Alice came for tea</u> as her mum was ill.	✓		

(1 mark: award 1 mark for all three correct)

19. (Despite) **(1 mark)**

20. Playtime lasts for 15 minutes. ✓

Playtime is in the morning. ✓

(1 mark: award 1 mark for both correct)

21. We're; haven't

(1 mark: award 1 mark for both correct)

22. Example: "Put on your coats and go out to play," said the teacher. **(1 mark)**

23. Examples: hairy; tall

(1 mark: award 1 mark for both correct)

24. Example: beautiful **(1 mark)**

25. Examples: Freya chose a book from the shelf. / Rachel planned to book the tickets later.

(1 mark: award 1 mark for two sentences using separate meanings of 'book')

26. After the race had finished, the two drivers shook hands.

The children filed into the classroom <u>because the bell had rung</u>.

<u>Although they were tired</u>, the children kept running.

(1 mark: award 1 mark for all three correct)

27. unattractive, unsightly ✓ **(1 mark)**

28. inactive; unstable; dissimilar

(1 mark: award 1 mark for all three correct)

29. break. ✓ **(1 mark)**

30. My brother – the one who is mad about music – is going to a music festival this weekend. **(1 mark)**

31. (-ly) **(1 mark)**

32. We had to buy the following: jam, butter, cream and scones. ✓ **(1 mark)**

33. We <u>were having</u> a great time in the swimming pool. **(1 mark)**

34. leaves; sheep; boxes; children

(1 mark: award 1 mark for all four correct)

35. bought; will catch

(1 mark: award 1 mark for both correct)

36.

Sentence	Apostrophe to show contraction	Apostrophe to show possession
Sam's bike was lying on the ground.		✓
You're all stars!	✓	
It was Ryan's turn next.		✓

(1 mark: award 1 mark for all three correct)

37. loudest – B (adjective);

lion – C (noun);

was – A (verb);

obviously – D (adverb)

(1 mark: award 1 mark for all four correct)

38. Example: I do not want any help. / I don't want any help. **(1 mark)**

39. Example: Do you fancy coming to mine for a party? **(1 mark)**

40. Natasha (my best friend) came to my house for a sleepover. ✓ **(1 mark)**

41. ate – eight; weight – wait; sail – sale

(1 mark: award 1 mark for all three correct)

42. (the;) (a;) (an)

(1 mark: award 1 mark for all three correct)

43. while ✓ **(1 mark)**

44. it; he **(1 mark: award 1 mark for both correct)**

45. Example: How often do you eat burgers? **(1 mark)**

46.

Sentence	Phrase	Clause
The old lady crossed the road.	✓	
They had fun <u>playing in the park</u>.		✓
The children ran <u>so they could stretch their legs</u>.		✓
The snake slithered <u>in his humid tank</u>.	✓	

(1 mark: award 1 mark for all four correct)

47. The bone was eaten by the dog. **(1 mark)**

48. The wind was very strong; the kite flew high in the sky. ✓ **(1 mark)**

49.

Sentence	After as a subordinating conjunction	After as a preposition
After I brushed my teeth, I went downstairs.	✓	
I ran after the bus but it didn't stop.		✓
After 9 o'clock we are ready to go to assembly.		✓

(1 mark: award 1 mark for all three correct)

50. If it <u>were</u> to rain, we would have to cancel the race. **(1 mark)**

Paper 2: spelling

These are the correct spellings:

1. flute
2. travelling
3. babies
4. hisses
5. destruction
6. calves
7. flour
8. interfere
9. elephant
10. business
11. cinema
12. hurried
13. discover
14. criticism
15. actually
16. abstract
17. hopping
18. geometry
19. stairs
20. parliament

Set B

Paper 1: questions

1. tie **(1 mark)**

2.

	Adverb	Adjective
happily	✓	
scary		✓

(1 mark: award 1 mark for both correct)

3. Mrs James is my teacher she makes learning fun. ✓ **(1 mark)**

4. (through) **(1 mark)**

5. **Example**: Would you like to go to the cinema today? **(1 mark)**

6. I have 15 different toys. ✓
My favourite toy is my Batman one. ✓
(1 mark: award 1 mark for both correct)

7. Ring me at home (you have my number) so we can chat. ✓ **(1 mark)**

8. How old are you?; Good gracious!; I am eight years old.
(1 mark: award 1 mark for all three correct)

9. In the first sentence, there are clearly three pastimes, with the comma separating 'cooking' and 'my pets'.
In the second sentence, it sounds like the person likes to cook his/her pets!
(1 mark: reference to both sentences will be awarded the mark)

10. Tidy your room! / Tidy your room. **(1 mark)**

11.

	Noun	Verb
to skip		✓
hoped		✓
car	✓	

(1 mark: award 1 mark for all three correct)

12. (larger) **(1 mark)**

13.

Sentence	Statement	Command	Question
Can you listen please			✓
I am listening to the teacher	✓		
Stop and listen		✓	

(1 mark: award 1 mark for all three correct)

14. We saw a man-eating shark at the aquarium. ✓
(1 mark)

15. jump, run; reverse; trips
(1 mark: award 1 mark for all three correct)

16. because; however; and
(1 mark: award 1 mark for all three correct)

17. built ✓ **(1 mark)**

18. me; me; me; I
(1 mark: award 1 mark for all four correct)

19. "When you are in a library," said the librarian, "you must be silent."
(1 mark: as long as inverted commas are correctly placed, other speech punctuation need not be included)

20. I she ✓ **(1 mark)**

21. **Fronted adverbial**: (Every day;) **adverb**: (hard)
(1 mark: award 1 mark for both correct)

22. The child jumped and screamed in anger. ✓
(1 mark)

23.

Sentence	Main clause	Subordinate clause	Relative clause
The animals stayed inside because it was snowing outside.		✓	
The baby, who was screaming loudly, would not go to sleep.			✓
Before school started, I went to the gym to do some exercise.	✓		
I cleaned up my bedroom, after my mum had asked me to.	✓		

(1 mark: award 1 mark for all four correct)

24. They're; won't **(1 mark)**

25. "How much further do I have to cycle?" moaned Tamzin. ✓ **(1 mark)**

26. Examples: shouted; announced; yelled; exclaimed **(1 mark)**

27. Examples: I gave her a ring and asked her to marry me. / I said I would ring her later.

(1 mark: award 1 mark for two sentences using separate meanings of the word 'ring')

28. mail – male; hole – whole; bear – bare

(1 mark: award 1 mark for all three correct)

29. fragile, delicate ✓ **(1 mark)**

30. excited – B (adjective);
child – C (noun);
talked – A (verb);
loudly – D (adverb)

(1 mark: award 1 mark for all four correct)

31. uneasy; immature; disagree

(1 mark: award 1 mark for all three correct)

32.

Sentence	Apostrophe to show contraction	Apostrophe to show possession
You'll need to work hard today!	✓	
I won't be able to help you.	✓	
Claire's work is the best!		✓

(1 mark: award 1 mark for all three correct)

33. The children, all aged four, went on a visit to the zoo. **(1 mark)**

34. Although Matilda's homework was <u>very</u> difficult, she produced a <u>really</u> excellent piece of writing.

(1 mark: award 1 mark for both correct)

35. Examples: friendly; childish; beautiful; crazy

(1 mark: all four correct for 1 mark)

36. I will be at football training at 9:00 am sharp. ✓

(1 mark)

37. When I wake up in the morning, I have a shower. After that I have my breakfast.

(1 mark: award 1 mark for one correctly placed comma, two correctly placed full stops and four correct capital letters)

38. We heard James sing on stage last week and have listened to <u>him</u> many times since. <u>He</u> is one of the best!

(1 mark: award 1 mark for both correct)

39. won't / mightn't **(1 mark)**

40. I should have done my homework last night.

(1 mark)

41. (The); (an); (a)

(1 mark: award 1 mark for all three correct)

42. In my bag I packed: a towel, a hairbrush, a swimming costume and a bottle of shampoo.

(1 mark: award 1 mark for one colon and two commas in the correct places)

43.

Sentence	Phrase	Clause
The news spread quickly on the internet.		✓
The noisy children played in the park.	✓	
To get away from the lion, the animals stampeded.		✓
The unhappy baby screamed in the wooden cot.	✓	

(1 mark: award 1 mark for all four correct)

44. It's been hot and sunny all day; we just hope it stays that way. **(1 mark)**

45. were **(1 mark)**

46. Examples: yours / his / hers **(1 mark)**

47. although **(1 mark)**

48. The circus's new show had to be cancelled. The children's disappointment was clear to see. Soon the children were walking home, holding their parents' hands.

(1 mark: award 1 mark for all three correct)

49. "Can you do an extra training session before the final?" asked our coach. **(1 mark)**

50. My mum's sister — currently working in the fashion industry — has met many celebrities. **(1 mark)**

Paper 2: spelling

These are the correct spellings:

1. heart
2. quicker
3. knight

4. exaggerated
5. animal
6. chutney
7. uncovered
8. symbols
9. halves
10. married
11. prism
12. abruptly
13. tomatoes
14. animation
15. stopped
16. kilometre
17. equalled
18. aisle
19. occupied
20. immediately

Set C

Paper 1: questions

1. (kind) (old) (uneven)
   (1 mark: award 1 mark for all three correct)
2. (Josh) (London) (Tuesday) (Samuel)

   Example: Josh. Because it is a proper noun or a name of a person. **(1 mark)**
3. I; I; me; me
   (1 mark: award 1 mark for all four correct)
4. "Do I have to go to school today?" moaned Simon. **(1 mark)**
5.

Sentence	Statement	Command	Question
I like eating pasta	✓		
Cook the pasta		✓	
Which pasta is your favourite			✓

   (1 mark: award 1 mark for all three correct)
6. pair; grown; bare
   (1 mark : award 1 mark for all three correct)
7. After dinner, we had a truly amazing dessert!
   (1 mark)
8. her   her ✓ **(1 mark)**
9. (mournfully) (angrily)
   (1 mark: award 1 mark for both correct)
10. run; ran; ran; ran
    (1 mark: award 1 mark for all four correct)
11. We packed lots of things (including the map) for our journey. ✓ **(1 mark)**

12.

	Verb	Adverb
shouted	✓	
loudly		✓
was	✓	

    (1 mark: award 1 mark for all three correct)
13. **Examples:** That really hurt! / What a lovely surprise! **(1 mark)**
14. (because) **(1 mark)**
15. (broke) (flew)
    (1 mark: award 1 mark for both correct)
16. I will run to school so that I will be early.; George will train / will be training hard.; The cows will jump over the moon!
    (1 mark: award 1 mark for all three correct)
17. The lions **are** eating their dinner; Brookside School **has** won the cup; Jason and I **have** fallen off our bikes.
    (1 mark: award 1 mark for all three correct)
18. Suddenly, there was silence in the stadium. ✓
    (1 mark)
19. **Examples:** the beautiful butterfly; the stormy sky
    (1 mark: award 1 mark for two correct phrases)
20. (Tim) (Chris) (Kierton) (Willowbank)
    (1 mark: award 1 mark for all four correct)
21. went – A (verb);
    happily – D (adverb);
    sunny – B (adjective);
    Spain – C (proper noun)
    (1 mark: award 1 mark for all four correct)
22. **Example:** The door creaked open slowly …
    (1 mark)
23. **Example:** Help me make the lunch! / Help me make the lunch.
    (1 mark: either exclamation mark or full stop is accepted)
24. The children were rescued by the firemen.
    (1 mark)
25. "I wish it was the end of school," whined Tom, "because I am going to play football."
    (1 mark)
26. **Example:** I am never going back. / I'm never going back.
    (1 mark: the sentence should not contain slang or double negatives)
27. dark, dreary ✓ **(1 mark)**

28. After a period of time, the sea calmed and the sun came out. **(1 mark)**

29.

Sentence	Apostrophe to show **contraction**	Apostrophe to show **possession**
Maya's coat is on the peg.		✓
Nick's digger is in the sandpit.		✓
They'll have to tidy up later!	✓	

(1 mark: award 1 mark for all three correct)

30.

Sentence	Main clause	Subordinate clause	Relative clause
My bike, which goes very fast, is shiny and new.			✓
My bike is shiny and new, although I know it won't be long before I scratch it!		✓	
My bike is shiny even though it is second-hand.	✓		

(1 mark: award 1 mark for all three correct)

31. To make the model I needed the following: glue, paint and card. ✓ **(1 mark)**

32. shouldn't; It'll **(1 mark)**

33. In my school bag, I have a maths book, a pencil case, a coat, a plastic frog and a pair of glasses.
(1 mark: award 1 mark for all four correct)

34. dreadful **(1 mark)**

35. (An) (The) (a)
(1 mark: award 1 mark for all three correct)

36. I am very hungry. ✓
Dinner is my favourite meal of the day. ✓
(1 mark: award 1 mark for both correct)

37. My friends (Jake and Max) came to my house for a sleepover. **(1 mark)**

38. Example: Who is the Prime Minister? **(1 mark)**

39. It had been many years since **O**xford had won the race. **T**hey have been working extra hard this year. **(1 mark: award 1 mark for two full stops and three capital letters)**

40. (in) **(1 mark)**

41. unafraid; discomfort; improbable
(1 mark: award 1 mark for all three correct)

42. don't **(1 mark)**

43.

Sentence	Phrase	Clause
The phone beeped in the silent room.	✓	
The mouse squeaked in his house.		✓
The quiet baby slept all day long.	✓	
They went into town so they could buy some food.		✓

(1 mark: award 1 mark for all four correct)

44. searched ✓ **(1 mark)**

45. I can't take you to your tennis lesson. ✓ **(1 mark)**

46. were **(1 mark)**

47. "You will find the museum at the end of the next road, on the left-hand side," said the boy. Or The boy said, "You will find the museum at the end of the next road, on the left-hand side." **(1 mark)**

48. Examples: circus, circumference
(1 mark: award 1 mark for two correct words)

49. My best friend – originally from Australia – knows lots of facts about wallabies. **(1 mark)**

50. aqua — water; bi — two; tele — distant; auto — self
(1 mark: award 1 mark for all four correct)

Paper 2: spelling

These are the correct spellings:

1. metre
2. thieves
3. secretary
4. donkeys
5. dancing
6. sweater
7. tomb
8. variety
9. quickest
10. twelfth
11. unnecessary
12. baptism
13. abnormally
14. carried
15. occurs
16. determined
17. saving
18. chopping
19. benefit
20. weight

Spelling test administration

The instructions below are for the spelling tasks.

Read the following instructions out to your child:

I am going to read some sentences out to you. Each sentence has a word missing. Listen carefully to the missing word and fill this in the answer space, making sure that you spell it correctly. I will read the word, then the word within the sentence, then I will repeat the word for a third time.

You should now read the spellings three times, as given below. Leave at least a 12-second gap between spellings. At the end, read all the sentences again, giving your child the chance to make any changes they wish to their answers.

Set A

Spelling 1: The word is **flute**.
I am learning to play the **flute**.
The word is **flute**.

Spelling 2: The word is **travelling**.
We were **travelling** on the train.
The word is **travelling**.

Spelling 3: The word is **babies**.
The **babies** were playing on
the carpet.
The word is **babies**.

Spelling 4: The word is **hisses**.
The snake **hisses** loudly in his tank.
The word is **hisses**.

Spelling 5: The word is **destruction**.
The explosion caused great
destruction.
The word is **destruction**.

Spelling 6: The word is **calves**.
The cow gave birth to two **calves**.
The word is **calves**.

Spelling 7: The word is **flour**.
Sam mixed **flour** into his cake mixture.
The word is **flour**.

Spelling 8: The word is **interfere**.
Max chose to **interfere** with Tom's
game.
The word is **interfere**.

Spelling 9: The word is **elephant**.
Freya's favourite animal at the zoo
was the **elephant**.
The word is **elephant**.

Spelling 10: The word is **business**.
The man had a very successful
business in the city.
The word is **business**.

Spelling 11: The word is **cinema**.
We watched the film at the **cinema**.
The word is **cinema**.

Spelling 12: The word is **hurried**.
The children **hurried** out to play.
The word is **hurried**.

Spelling 13: The word is **discover**.
Howard Carter was proud to
discover the tomb.
The word is **discover**.

Spelling 14: The word is **criticism**.
The children responded to the
criticism by improving their work.
The word is **criticism**.

Spelling 15: The word is **actually**.
Superman was **actually** Clark Kent.
The word is **actually**.

Spelling 16: The word is **abstract**.
My uncle went to an exhibition of
abstract paintings.
The word is **abstract**.

Spelling 17: The word is **hopping**.
Matilda won the **hopping** race on
sports day.
The word is **hopping**.

Spelling 18: The word is **geometry**.
The children were learning about
geometry in maths.
The word is **geometry**.

Spelling 19: The word is **stairs**.
Mark ran quickly up the **stairs**.
The word is **stairs**.

Spelling 20: The word is **parliament**.
The **parliament** building is in
London.
The word is **parliament**.

Set B

Spelling 1: The word is **heart**.
The **heart** pumps blood around
the body.
The word is **heart**.

Spelling 2: The word is **quicker**.
The hare is **quicker** than the tortoise.
The word is **quicker**.

Spelling 3: The word is **knight**.
Sir Lancelot was a brave **knight**.
The word is **knight**.

Spelling 4: The word is **exaggerated**.
The fisherman **exaggerated** the size
of the fish he caught.
The word is **exaggerated**.

Spelling 5: The word is **animal**.
The elephant is a large **animal**.
The word is **animal**.

Spelling 6: The word is **chutney**.
I made green tomato **chutney** to
have with cheese.
The word is **chutney**.

Spelling 7: The word is **uncovered**.
The plot to rob the bank was
uncovered by the police.
The word is **uncovered**.

Spelling 8: The word is **symbols**.
To read a map successfully, you need
to know what the **symbols** mean.
The word is **symbols**.

Spelling 9: The word is **halves**.
Two **halves** make a whole.
The word is **halves**.

Spelling 10: The word is **married**.
The couple **married** in a church.
The word is **married**.

Spelling 11: The word is **prism**. A **prism** is a 3-D shape. The word is **prism**.

Spelling 12: The word is **abruptly**. Matthew's car stopped **abruptly**. The word is **abruptly**.

Spelling 13: The word is **tomatoes**. Ian was proud of the **tomatoes** he had grown. The word is **tomatoes**.

Spelling 14: The word is **animation**. Wallace and Gromit is a funny **animation**. The word is **animation**.

Spelling 15: The word is **stopped**. The children **stopped** talking when the teacher entered the room. The word is **stopped**.

Spelling 16: The word is **kilometre**. There are 1,000 metres in a **kilometre**. The word is **kilometre**.

Spelling 17: The word is **equalled**. The athlete **equalled** the world record in the 100 m sprint. The word is **equalled**.

Spelling 18: The word is **aisle**. The shop assistant had to clean up a spillage in the drinks **aisle**. The word is **aisle**.

Spelling 19: The word is **occupied**. The ladies' toilet was already **occupied**. The word is **occupied**.

Spelling 20: The word is **immediately**. The baby **immediately** started to cry when she was put to bed. The word is **immediately**.

Set C

Spelling 1: The word is **metre**. The children used a **metre** stick to draw a line. The word is **metre**.

Spelling 2: The word is **thieves**. The **thieves** dropped the stolen vase in their rush to escape. The word is **thieves**.

Spelling 3: The word is **secretary**. The school **secretary** welcomed the visitors. The word is **secretary**.

Spelling 4: The word is **donkeys**. A line of **donkeys** were led along the beach. The word is **donkeys**.

Spelling 5: The word is **dancing**. Margaret enjoys ballroom **dancing**. The word is **dancing**.

Spelling 6: The word is **sweater**. I bought a green **sweater** for my father. The word is **sweater**.

Spelling 7: The word is **tomb**. Howard Carter entered the **tomb** cautiously. The word is **tomb**.

Spelling 8: The word is **variety**. She bought a **variety** pack of crisps. The word is **variety**.

Spelling 9: The word is **quickest**. Flying is the **quickest** way to travel to New York from England. The word is **quickest**.

Spelling 10: The word is **twelfth**. I was the **twelfth** child in my class to get chickenpox. The word is **twelfth**.

Spelling 11: The word is **unnecessary**. Shoes are **unnecessary** on the beach. The word is **unnecessary**.

Spelling 12: The word is **baptism**. The church service included a **baptism**. The word is **baptism**.

Spelling 13: The word is **abnormally**. The giraffe has an **abnormally** long neck. The word is **abnormally**.

Spelling 14: The word is **carried**. Philip **carried** his bag home from school. The word is **carried**.

Spelling 15: The word is **occurs**. Your birthday **occurs** on the same date every year. The word is **occurs**.

Spelling 16: The word is **determined**. They were **determined** to reach the South Pole. The word is **determined**.

Spelling 17: The word is **saving**. Jemima was **saving** her pocket money to buy an action figure. The word is **saving**.

Spelling 18: The word is **chopping**. Grandpa was **chopping** wood for the fire. The word is **chopping**.

Spelling 19: The word is **benefit**. Children **benefit** from regular exercise. The word is **benefit**.

Spelling 20: The word is **weight**. Paul staggered under the **weight** of the suitcase. The word is **weight**.